CW00419984

AIRLINE TAIL
COLOURS

Gerry Manning

MIDLAND

Introduction

This book is the fourth edition of the title; its aim is to show the tail colours of airlines, large and small, including air taxi operators and government flights with a worldwide coverage.

It is quite common today for some carriers to have multiple tail markings; these include *jetBlue* with different designs around a common theme, *Frontier Airlines* with different animals and birds and *Air India Express* with art and views from that country. Examples of alternative designs are shown for many of the carriers.

The 'retro' colour scheme is also a growing trend where an airline paints one example of their fleet in the livery they used in the 1950s or 60s. Again, examples are included alongside the main entry.

It is also a fact of life that airlines go out of business, change names or merge following takeovers. By the time this book is published a number of carriers illustrated will have ceased operations.

Many of the airlines of the world have banded together into loose associations to offer seamless travel between cities on different continents, with each carrier running as an individual company but offering connections with the others. The three main ones are Star Alliance, One-World and Sky Team. Each airline usually paints one or more of their fleet in a special livery to show that they are part of one of these three groups.

Acknowledgements

I would like to thank Bob O'Brien and John Smith for the use of a number of photographs that filled the gaps in my own travels.

Airline Tail Colours
Gerry Manning

First published 2012

ISBN 978 1 85780 350 1

Published by Ian Allan Publishing
an imprint of Ian Allan Publishing Ltd, Hersham, Surrey, KT12 4RG.

Printed in England by Ian Allan Printing Ltd, Hersham, Surrey KT12 4RG.
Visit the Ian Allan Publishing website at
www.ianallanpublishing.com
Distributed in the United States of America and Canada by BookMasters Distribution Services.

The name of the airline

Base city of the airline

Turkish Airlines

TK/THY | Istanbul – Ataturk | Turkey = TC

Retro scheme

Nationality of carrier and the registration prefix of that nation.
NB. With the common practice of airlines leasing aircraft rather than to purchase them the registration seen on the aeroplane does not always relate to the operating country but to the domain of the leasing organisation.

The three-letter ICAO code (International Civil Aviation Organisation) airline designator.
NB. Some carriers have none or only one.

The two-letter IATA code (International Air Transport Association) airline designator.

Abbe Air

Wasilla | USA = N

Ades
Aerolineas del Este Ltda

Villavicencio | Colombia = HK

Adlair Aviation

Cambridge Bay | Canada = C

Aerosur

5L/RSU | Santa Cruz | Bolivia = CP

Adria Airways

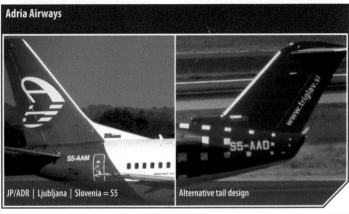

JP/ADR | Ljubljana | Slovenia = S5

Alternative tail design

4

Aero Republica

P5/RPB | Bogota | Colombia = HK

Aerovanguardia

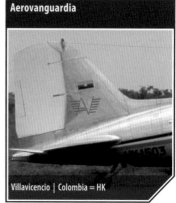

Villavicencio | Colombia = HK

Aerosucre Colombia

/KRE | Bogota | Colombia = HK

Aerotaca

/ATK | Bogota | Colombia = HK

Aerogal
Aerolineas Galapagos SA

/KRE | Bogota | Colombia = HK

Aero Dienst

/ADN | Nuremberg | Germany = D

Aer Arran

RE/REA | Dublin | Ireland = EI

Aer Lingus

EI/EIN | Dublin | Ireland = EI

Aerolineas Argentinas

AR/ARG | Buenos Aires | Argentina = LV

Aeromas

/MSM | Montevideo | Uruguay = CX

AeroCondor SAC

Q6/CDP | Lima | Peru = OB

Aero Asia

E4/RSO | Karachi | Pakistan = AP

Aero Mexico

AM/AMX | Mexico City | Mexico = XA/B/C

Aeroflot – Russian Airlines

SU/AFL | Moscow | Russia = RA

Aeroflot Nord
Nordavia Regional Airlines

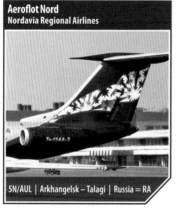

5N/AUL | Arkhangelsk – Talagi | Russia = RA

Aeroflot – Don (Donavia)

D9 /DNV | Rostov-on-Don | Russia = RA

Aegean Airlines

A3/AEE | Athens | Greece = SX

Aerosvit Airlines

VV/AEW | Kiev – Borispol | Ukraine = UR

Afriqiyah Airways

8U/AAW | Tripoli | Libya = 5A

African Charter Airline

Johannesburg | South Africa = ZS

Airbus Transport International

/BGA | Toulouse – Blagnac | France = F

Airnet Express

/USC | Columbus | USA = N

Aires
Aerovias de Intergracion Regional SA

4C/ARE | Bogota | Colombia = HK

Aliansa
Aerolineas Andinas SA

Villavicencio | Colombia = HK

Aigle Azur

ZI/AAF | Paris Orly | France = F

Al Khayala

Jeddah | Saudi Arabia = HZ

Allegiant Air

G4/AAY | Las Vegas | USA = N

Alitalia

AZ/AZA | Rome Fiumicino | Italy = I

Alliance Avia

St Petersburg Pulkovo & Rzhevka | Russia = RA

Alrosa Mirny Air Enterprises

6R/DRU | Mirny | Russia = RA

Alaska Airlines

AS/ASA | Seattle/Tacoma | USA = N

Extra tail marks 'garland'

'Wild Alaska Seafood' scheme

'Make a wish' scheme

American Airlines

Dallas/Fort Worth | USA = N

'Support the Troops' special tail colours

American Eagle Airlines

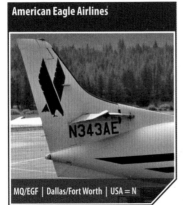

MQ/EGF | Dallas/Fort Worth | USA = N

Albanian Airlines

LV/LBC | Tirana | Albania = ZA

Alliance Airlines

QQ/FWQ | Brisbane | Australia = VH

AMC Aviation

YJ/AMV | Cairo | Egypt = SU

Amsterdam Airlines

WD/AAN | Amsterdam Schiphol | Holland = PH

Anadolujet

Ankara | Turkey = TC

All Nippon Airways

NH/ANH | Tokyo Haneda | Japan = JA

'Pocket Monsters' scheme

'Pokémon' scheme

Australian Air Express

XM/XME | Melbourne | Australia = VH

Augsburg Airways

IQ/AUB | Augsburg | Germany = D

Aurela

/LSK | Vilnius | Lithuania = LY

Air Nippon

EL/ANK | Tokyo Haneda | Japan = JA

'Super Dolphin' scheme

Austrian Airlines

OE-LBN

OS/AUA | Vienna | Austria = OE

OE-LBU

'Football' special scheme

Austrian Arrows
Operated by Tyrolean Airways

OE-

VO/TYR | Innsbruck | Austria = OE

Aurigny Air Service

G-BXTN

.com

Guernsey Channel Islands | UK = G

Austral Lineas Aereas

AU/AUT | Buenos Aires – Aeroparque Jorge Newbery | Argentina = LV

Avianca

AV/AVA | Bogota | Colombia = HK

Aviaenergo

7U/ERG | Moscow – Sheremetyevo | Russia = RA

Aviastar TU

4B/TUP | Moscow – Zhukovsky | Russia = RA

Aviation Australia

Eagle Farm | Australia = VH

Armavia

U8/RNV | Yerevan | Armenia = EK

Aria Air

/IRX | Lar | Iran = EP

Arkefly

OR/TFL | Amsterdam Schiphol | Holland = PH

Arctic Sunwest

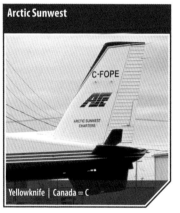

Yellowknife | Canada = C

Arkia Israeli Airlines

IZ/AIZ | Tel Aviv | Israel = 4X

Astraeus Airlines

5W/AEU | London – Gatwick | UK = G

Asiana Airlines

OZ/AAR | Seoul | Korea = HL

Atlas Air

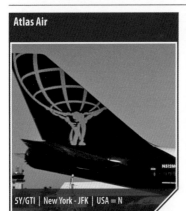

5Y/GTI | New York - JFK | USA = N

Atlantic Airlines

/NPT | Coventry | UK = G

Aero Transporte SA

/AMP | Lima | Peru = OB

Asiana Airlines (Cargo)

OZ/AAR | Seoul | Korea = HL

Atlas Blue

8A/BMM | Marrakech | Morocco = CN

Atlasjet Airlines

KK/KKK | Antalya | Turkey = TC

Atlant Soyuz

3G/AYZ | Moscow Vnukovo | Russia = RA

Alternative tail colours

Azerbaijan Hava Yollari

J2/AHY | Baku | Azerbaijan = 4K

Air Astana

KC/KZR | Astana | Kazakhstan = UP

Air Algerie

AH/DAH | Algiers | Algeria = 7T

Air Arctic

Fairbanks | USA = N

Air Baltic

BT/BTI | Riga | Latvia = YL

Special 'Dancer' scheme

Air Arabia

G9/ABY | Sharjah | UAE = A6

Air Blue

ED/ABQ | Karachi | Pakistan = AP

Air Botswana

BP/BOT | Gaborone | Botswana = A2

Air Berlin

AB/BER | Berlin – Tegel | Germany = D

Air Colombia

Villavicencio | Colombia = HK

Air Caraibes

TX/FWI | Pointe-a-Pitre Guadeloupe
| French Overseas = F-O

AirBridge Cargo

RU/ABW | Moscow – Sheremetyevo
| Russia = RA

Air Comet

A7/MPD | Madrid – Barajas | Spain = EC

Air Calin

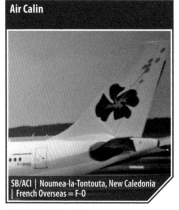

SB/ACI | Noumea-la-Tontouta, New Caledonia
| French Overseas = F-O

Air Caledonia

TY/TPC | Noumea-Magenta, New Caledonia
| French Overseas = F-O

Air Canada

AC/ACA | Montreal – Trudeau | Canada = C   Retro 'Trans-Canada Air Lines' scheme

Air China

CA/CCA | Beijing | China = B

Air Dolomiti

EN/DLA | Verona | Italy = I

Air Europa

UX/AEA | Palma | Spain = EC

Air Finland

OF/FIF | Helsinki – Vantaa | Finland = OH

Air Grand Canyon

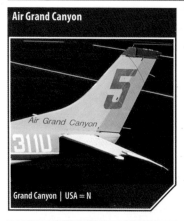

Grand Canyon | USA = N

Air Italy

I9/ | Milan – Malpensa | Italy = I

Air India

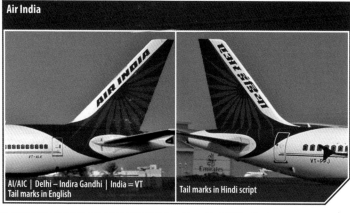

AI/AIC | Delhi – Indira Gandhi | India = VT
Tail marks in English

Tail marks in Hindi script

Air France

AF/AFR | Paris Orly | France = F

Air Jamaica

JM/AJM | Kingston – Norman Manley
| Jamaica = 6Y

Air India Express

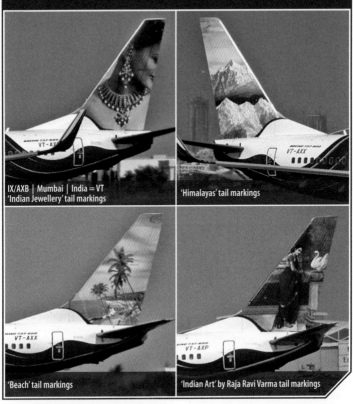

IX/AXB | Mumbai | India = VT
'Indian Jewellery' tail markings

'Himalayas' tail markings

'Beach' tail markings

'Indian Art' by Raja Ravi Varma tail markings

Air Koryo

JS/KOR | Pyongyang | North Korea = P

Airlinair

Chaque région est capitale

A5/RLA | Paris – Orly | France = F

Air Lazur

/LZR | Sofia | Bulgaria = LZ

Air Malawi

QM/AML | Blantyre | Malawi = 7Q

Air Memphis

/MHS | Cairo | Egypt = SU

Air Malta

KM/AMC | Malta – Luqa | Malta = 9H

Air Macau

NX/AMU | Macau | China Macau = B-M

Air Mediterranee

ML/BIE | Toulouse – Blagnac | France = F

Air Moldova

9U/MLD | Chisinau | Moldova = ER

Air Mauritius

MK/MAU | Mauritius | Mauritius = 3B

Air North Airlines

4N/ANT | Whitehorse | Canada = C

Air Namibia

SW/NMB | Windhoek – Eros | Namibia = V5

Air Niugini

PX/ANG | Port Moresby
| Papua New Guinea = P2

Air New Zealand

NZ/ANZ | Auckland | New Zealand = ZK

Air Nelson
New Zealand Link

ZK-FXQ

/RLK | Nelson | New Zealand = ZK

Air One

AP/ADH | Rome Fiumicino
& Milan Linate | Italy = I

Air Prishtina

Zurich | Switzerland = HB

Air Pacific

Fiji

DQ-FJF

FJ/FJI | Nadi | Fiji = DQ

Air Plus Comet

A7/MPD | Madrid – Barajas | Spain = EC

Airquarius Aviation

EAS

Executive Avionic
Solutions

ZS-JAV

/AQU | Johannesburg – Lanseria
| South Africa = ZS

25

Air Saint-Pierre

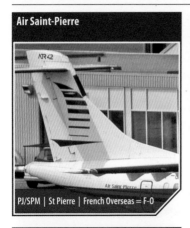

PJ/SPM | St Pierre | French Overseas = F-O

Air Southwest

SZ/WOW | Plymouth | UK = G

Air Tindi

8T/ | Yellowknife | Canada = C

Air Tahiti Nui

TN/THT | Papeete – Faa'a | French Overseas = F-O

airTran Airways

FL/TRS | Atlanta- Hartsfield | USA = N

Air Transat

TS/TSC | Montreal – Trudeau | Canada = C

Air Union
Amalgam of several airlines

Various bases | Russia = RA

Air Zimbabwe

UM/AZW | Harare | Zimbabwe = Z

Baxter Aviation

Nanaimo Sea Plane Base | Canada = C

British Airways

BA/BAW | London – Heathrow | UK = G

Baboo

F7/BBO | Geneva | Switzerland = HB

Bangkok Airways

PG/BKP | Bangkok | Thailand = HS

Bahrain Air

2B/BAB | Bahrain International
| Bahrain = A9C

Bahrain Royal Flight

/BAH | Bahrain International | Bahrain = A9C

Baja Air

Aurora | USA = N

Batavia Air

7P/BTV | Jakarta – Soekarno Hatta
International | Indonesia = PK

Bearskin Airlines

JV/BLS | Sioux Lookout | Canada = C

Berkut Air Services

/BEK | Almaty | Kazakhstan = UP

Belair Airlines

4T/BHP | Zurich | Switzerland = HB

Belle Air

LZ/LBY | Tirana | Albania = ZA

Belavia

EW-85706

B2/BRU | Minsk | Belarus = EW

BH Air
Balkan Holidays Airline

BHAir

/BGH | Sofia | Bulgaria = LZ

Binter Canarias

EC-IZO

NT/IBB | Las Palmas – Grand Canaria
| Spain = EC

Biman Bangladesh Airlines

BG/BBC | Dhaka | Bangladesh = S2

Blue Bird Aviation

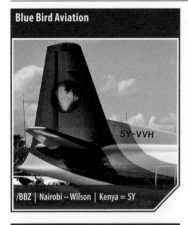

5Y-VVH

/BBZ | Nairobi – Wilson | Kenya = 5Y

Blue 1

Blue 1.

OH-SAL

KF/KFB | Helsinki – Vantaa | Finland = OH

Blue Sky Airlines

EP-N

/BLM | Yerevan | Armenia = EK

Blue Line

4Y/BLE | Paris – Charles De Gaulle | France = F

Blue Panorama Airlines

EI-CUA

BV/BPA | Rome – Fiumicino | Italy = I

Blue Air Transport Aerian

Blue Air
web.com

YR-BIC

OB/JOR | Bucharest – Baneasa Aurel Vlaicu
| Romania = YR

bmibaby

WW/BMI | East Midlands | UK = G

bmi

BD/BMA | East Midlands | UK =G

British Gulf International

/BGI | Sharjah | UAE = A6 (Fleet registered in Sao Tome & Principe = S9)

Brussels Airlines

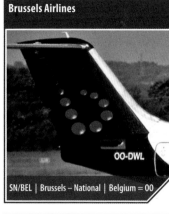

SN/BEL | Brussels -- National | Belgium = OO

Brooks Fuel

Fairbanks | USA = N

Bush Air cargo

Anchorage International | USA = N

Bulgaria Air

FB/LZB | Sofia | Bulgaria = LZ

Bulgarian Air Charter

Sofia | Bulgaria = LZ

Bylina

/BYL | Moscow – Bykovo | Russia = RA

Buraq Air

UZ/BRQ | Tripoli – Mitiga | Libya = 5A

Buffalo Airways

J4/BFL | Yellowknife | Canada = C

China Postal Airlines

8Y/CYZ | Tianjin | China = B

Cimber Sterling

QI/ | Sonderborg | Denmark =OY
Showing own tail markings

Showing SAS tail markings.
Operates feeder services

China Southern Airlines

CZ/CSN | Beijing – Capital | China = B

City Airlines

CF/SDR | Gothenburg – Landvetter
| Sweden = SE

Cielos del Peru

A2/CIU | Lima | Peru = OB

Cirrus Airlines

C9/RUS | Mannheim | Germany = D

Clickair

XG/CLI | Barcelona – El Prat | Spain = EC

Colgan Air

9L/CJC | Memphis | USA = N

Courtesy Air

Buffalo Narrows | Canada = C

Copa Airlines
Companie Panamena de Aviacion SA

CM/CMP | Panama –Tocumen International | Panama = HP

Continental Airlines

CO/COA | Houston – George Bush | USA = N

Columbia Helicopters

/WCO | Aurora State | USA = N

Contact Air Flugdienst

C3/KIS | Stuttgart | Germany = D
Lufthansa Regional scheme

Conair Aviation

/CRC | Abbotsford | Canada = C

Comlux Aviation

/MLM | Malta – Luqa | Malta = 9H

Coulson Aircrane

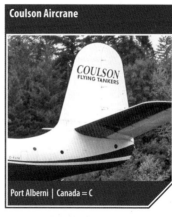

Port Alberni | Canada = C

Corendon Air

7H/CAI | Antalya International | Turkey = TC   Alternative scheme

CAA
Compagnie Africaine d'Aviation

Kinshasa – Ndolo | Congo – Kinshasa = 9Q

Cardig Air

8F/CAD | Jakarta – Soekarno Hatta
International | Indonesia = PK

Cargojet Airways

W8/CJT | Hamilton | Canada = C

Carpatair

V3/KRP | Timisoara | Romania = YR

Canadian North

5T/MPE | Yellowknife | Canada = C

Central Mountain Air

9M/GLR | Smithers | Canada = C

Cathay Pacific Airways

CX/CPA | Hong Kong International
| China Hong Kong = B-H

CargoLux Airlines

CV/CLX | Luxembourg | Luxembourg = LX

Caspian Airlines

RV/CPN | Tehran – Mehrabad | Iran = EP

Central Wings

CO/CLW | Warsaw –Okecie | Poland = SP

Centre-Avia

J7/CVC | Moscow – Bykovo | Russia = RA

Cebu Pacific

5J/CEB | Manila | Philippines = RP

China Airlines

CI/CAL | Taipei | China – Taiwan = B

China Xinhua Airlines

XW/CXH | Beijing – Capital | China = B

China Eastern Airlines

MU/CES | Shanghai – Hongqiao | China = B

China Cargo Airlines

CK/CKK | Shanghai – Hongqiao | China = B
Division of China Eastern

CHC Helicopters

Cape Town | South Africa = ZS

Chanchangi Airlines

5B/NCH | Kaduna | Nigeria = 5N

38

Condor Flugdienst

DE/CFG | Frankfurt | Germany = D

Special scheme

Condor Berlin

/CIB | Berlin – Schoenefeld | Germany = D

Croatia Airlines

OU/CTN | Zagreb | Croatia = 9A

Cubana

CU/CUB | Havana – Jose Marti International | Cuba = CU

Cyprus Airways

CY/CYP | Larnaca | Cyprus = 5B

Czech Airlines

OK/CSA | Prague – Ruzyne
| Czech Republic = OK

Special markings 'Holiday Aircraft'

Continental Airways

PC/PVV | Moscow – Sheremetyevo
| Russia = RA

Chang An Airlines

2Z/CGN | Xian – Xianyang | China = B

Cityjet

WX/BCY | Dublin | Ireland = EI

Cygnus Air
Now Gestair Cargo

/RGN | Madrid – Barajas | Spain = EC

Delta Air Lines

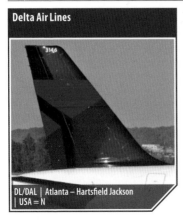

DL/DAL | Atlanta – Hartsfield Jackson | USA = N

Dagestan Airlines

N2/DAG | Makhachkala | Russia = RA

Darwin Airline

0D/DWT | Lugano – Agno | Switzerland = HB

Danube Wings

V5/VPA | Bratislava – M R Stefanik | Slovakia = OM

Dexter Air Taxi

Moscow – Bykovo | Russia = RA

Dniproavia

Z6/UDN | Dnepropetrovsk | Ukraine = UR

Druk Air

KB/DRK | Paro | Bhutan = A5

Dalavia – Far East Airways

RA-86560

H8/KHB | Khabarovsk – Novy | Russia = RA

Deutsche Lufthansa Berlin – Stiftung

JUNKERS

D-CDLH

Hamburg | Germany = D

Dragonair

KA/HDA | Hong Kong International
| China – Hong Kong = B-H

DSA

DSA

Hradec Kralove | Czech Republic = OK

East African Safari Air

5Y-QQQ

B5/EXZ | Nairobi – Wilson | Kenya = 5Y

easyJet

U2/EZY | London – Luton | UK = G

Edelweiss Air

WK/EDW | Zurich | Switzerland = HB

Eastern Airways

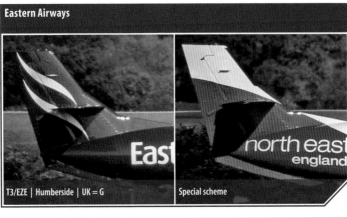

T3/EZE | Humberside | UK = G

Special scheme

Egyptair

MS/MSR | Cairo International | Egypt = SU

Alternative scheme

Egyptair Express

MS/MSE | Cairo International | Egypt = SU

EG & G Flight Operations

Las Vegas – McCarran | USA = N

El Al Israel Airlines

LY/ELY | Tel Aviv – Ben Gurion | Israel = 4X

Emirates

EK/UAE | Dubai | UAE = A6

Eram Air

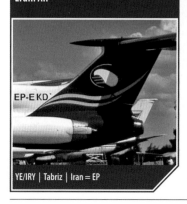

YE/IRY | Tabriz | Iran = EP

Ethiopian Airlines

ET/ETH | Addis Ababa | Ethiopia = ET

Estonian Air

OV/ELL | Tallinn – Ylemiste | Estonia = ES

ERA Aviation

7H/ERH | Anchorage International | USA = N

Etihad Airways

EY/ETD | Abu Dhabi International | UAE = A6

EuroCypria Airlines

UI/ECA | Larnaca | Cyprus = 5B

Euro Atlantic Airways

MM/MMZ | Lisbon | Portugal = CS

EuroLot

K2/ELO | Warsaw – Frederic Chopin | Poland = SP

Europe Airpost

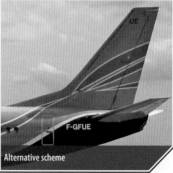

50/FPO | Paris – Charles De Gaulle | France = F

Alternative scheme

Eurowings

EW/EWG | Nuremberg | Germany = D

Everts Air Alaska

/VTS | Fairbanks International | USA = N

Eva Air

BR/EVA | Taipei –Taoyuan International
| China – Taiwan = B

Expo Aviation

8D/EXV | Colombo – Bandaranayike
International | Sri Lanka = 4R

Express Jet

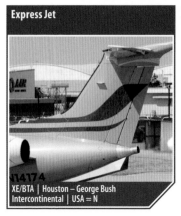

XE/BTA | Houston – George Bush
Intercontinental | USA = N

Exin

/EXN | Katowice | Poland = SP

Fair

FW/IBX | Osaka – Itami | Japan = JA
Now fly as Ibex Airlines

Farnair Switzerland

/FAT | Basel/Mulhouse – Euroairport
| Switzerland = HB

Fars Air

QE/QFZ | Qeshm | Iran = EP

Federal Express

FX/FDX | Memphis International | USA = N

Finnair

AY/FIN | Helsinki – Vantaa | Finland = OH

Special retro scheme

flyBe

BE/BEE | Exeter | UK = G

Special scheme

Finn Comm Airlines

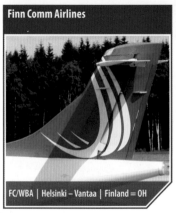

FC/WBA | Helsinki – Vantaa | Finland = OH

First Air

7F/FAB | Kanata | Canada = C

First Nations Transportation

Gimli | Canada = C

Flair Airlines

/FLE | Kelowna | Canada = C

flyLAL Charters

Vilnius | Lithuania = LY

Frontier Airlines

F9/FFT | Denver International | USA = N

Alternative tail markings

Alternative tail markings

Fly540

5H/FFV | Nairobi – Jomo Kenyatta International | Kenya = 5Y

Freebird Airlines

FH/FHY | Istanbul – Ataturk | Turkey = TC

Futura International Airways

FH/FUA | Palma – Son Sant Joan | Spain = EC

Fugro Airborne Surveys

Ottawa | Canada = C

Gabon Airlines

GY/GBK | Libreville | Gabon = TR

Garuda Indonesia Airways

GA/GIA | Jakarta – Soekarno Hatta International | Indonesia = PK

Groznyavia

/GOZ | Grozny | Russia = RA

Globus

GH/GLP | Moscow – Domodedovo
| Russia = RA

Gazpromavia

4G/GZP | Moscow – Vnukovo | Russia = RA

Germanwings

4U/GWI | Cologne | Germany = D

Special scheme

Special scheme

Germania Flug

ST/GMI | Berlin – Schoenefeld | Germany = D

GMG Airlines

Z5/ | Dhaka | Bangladesh = S2

Georgian Airways

A9/TGZ | Tbilisi International | Georgia = 4L

Grand Canyon Airlines

/CVU | Grand Canyon | USA = N

Grand China Express Air

GS/GCR | Tianjin Binhai International
| China = B

Great Wall Airlines

IJ/GWL | Shanghai – Pudong | China = B

Gulf Air

GF/GFA | Bahrain International | Bahrain = A9C

Hawkair Aviation Services

BH/ | Terrace | Canada = C

Harbour Air

H3/ | Vancouver International | Canada = C

Hokkaido International Airlines
Air Do

HD/ADO | Sapporo – Chitose | Japan = JA

Hainan Airlines

HU/CHH | Haikou – Meilan International | China = B

Hamburg International Airlines

4R/HHI | Hamburg – Fuhlsbuttel | Germany = D

Hawaiian Airlines

HA/HAL | Honolulu International | USA = N

Hewa Bora Airways

EO/ALX | Kinshasa – N'Djili
| Congo Kinshasa = 9Q

Hola Airlines

H5/HOA | Palma – Son Sant Joan | Spain = EC

Hello

HW/FHE | Basel/Mulhouse Euroairport
| Switzerland = HB

Helvetic Airways

2L/OAW | Zurich | Switzerland = HB

Alternative scheme

Hong Kong Airlines

HX/CRK | Hong Kong
| Hong Kong – China = B-H

Horizon Air

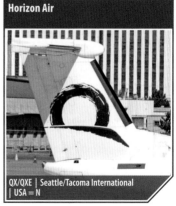

QX/QXE | Seattle/Tacoma International
| USA = N

Indian Airlines

VT-EPJ

IC/IAC | Delhi – Indira Gandhi International
| India = VT

Iberia

JRE

IB/IBE | Madrid – Barajas | Spain = EC

Icaro SA

EAFAIR

X8/ICD | Quito | Ecuador = HC

Iberworld

TY/IWD | Palma – Son Sant Joan | Spain = EC

Icelandair

FI/ICE | Keflavik | Iceland = TF

Interair

D6/ILN | Johannesburg | South Africa = ZS

Infinity Flight Services

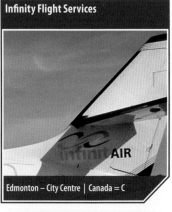

Edmonton – City Centre | Canada = C

Intal Air

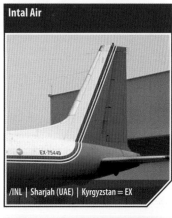

/INL | Sharjah (UAE) | Kyrgyzstan = EX

Intercontinental De Aviacion

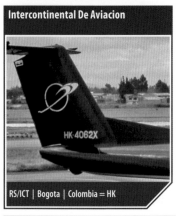

RS/ICT | Bogota | Colombia = HK

Intersky Luftfahrt

3L/ISK | Friedrichshafen – Loewental | Austria = OE

Iran Air

IR/IRA | Tehran – Mehrabad International
| Iran = EP

Alternative tail scheme

Itek Air

EX-311

GI/IKA | Bishkek | Kyrgyzstan = EX

Israir

4X-ABC

6H/ISR | Tel Aviv –Sde Dov | Israel = 4X

Iran Aseman Airlines

-ASC

EP/IRC | Tehran – Mehrabad International
| Iran = EP

J-Air

JA204J

/JLG | Hiroshima | Japan = JA

Japan Air Commuter

JA8642

3X/JAC | Kagoshima | Japan = JA

Japan Airlines International

JA8905

JL/JAL | Tokyo – Narita & Haneda | Japan = JA

Japan Transocean Air

JA8940

NU/JTA | Okinawa – Naha | Japan = JA

Jazeera Airways

9K-

J9/JZR | Kuwait | Kuwait = 9K

JAL Express

JA8994

JC/JEX | Osaka – Itami | Japan = JA

JA8994

Special scheme

Jazz (Air Canada)

QK/JZA | Halifax | Canada = C

Alternative coloured tail

Jet Time

/JTG | Copenhagen – Kastrup | Denmark = OY

Jet Airways

9W/JAI | Mumbai | India = VT

Jetstar Asia Airways

3K/JSA | Singapore – Changi | Singapore = 9V

Jet2.com

LS/EXS | Leeds/Bradford | UK = G

jetBlue Airways

B6/JBU | New York – JFK | USA = N

10th anniversary commemorative tail scheme

Jet Air

O2/JEA | Warsaw – Frederic Chopin
| Poland = SP

JAT Airways

JU/JAT | Belgrade – Surcin | Serbia = YU

Johnsons Air

/JON | Accra | Ghana = 9G

JU-Air

Duebendorf | Switzerland = HB

Kalitta Air

K4/CKS | Detroit – Willow Run | USA = N

Kam Air

RQ/KMF | Kabul | Afghanistan = YA

Kartika Airlines

PK-KAO

3Y/KAE | Jakarta – Soekarno Hatta
International | Indonesia = PK

Kayala Airline

XY/KNE | Jeddah | Saudi Arabia = HZ

Karthago Airlines

5R/KAJ | Djerba | Tunisia = TS

KD Air Corp.

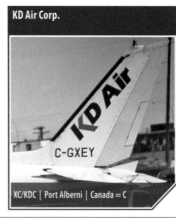

C-GXEY

XC/KDC | Port Alberni | Canada = C

Kelowna Flightcraft Group

KW/KFA | Kelowna | Canada = C

Kenn Borek Air

4K/KBA | Calgary – Springbank | Canada = C

Kenya Airways

KQ/KQA | Nairobi – Jomo Kenyatta International | Kenya = 5Y

Kingfisher Airlines

IT/KFR | Mumbai | India = VT

Kish Air

Y9/IRK | Tehran – Mehrabad International | Iran = EP

Komas Air

/KMG | Belgrade – Nikola Tesla | Serbia = YU

Kenmore Air Express

MS/KEN | Kenmore Sea Plane Base | USA = N

Special tail markings

Special tail markings

Korean Air

KE/KAL | Seoul – Incheon | Korea = HL

Koral Blue

/KBR | Sharm el Sheikh | Egypt = SU

Kolavia

7K/KGL | Surgut | Russia = RA

KLM Royal Dutch Airlines

KL/KLM | Amsterdam – Schiphol | Holland = PH

'Cargo' tail markings

'KLM Asia' tail markings

'Retro' scheme

Skyteam tail markings

Komos

/KSM | Moscow – Vnukovo | Russia = RA

Kibris Turkish Airlines

YK/KYV | Ercan | Turkish Republic of Northern Cyprus = TC

Kras Air

7B/KJC | Krasnoyarsk | Russia = RA

Kuban Airlines

GW/KIL | Krasnodar | Russia = RA

Kulula.com

MN/CAW | Johannesburg International | South Africa = ZS

Kuwait Airways

KU/KAC | Kuwait | Kuwait = 9K

LAT Charter

6Y/LTC | Riga | Latvia = YL

Lineas Aereas Suramericanas

/LAU | Bogota | Colombia = HK

Linhas Aereas de Mocambique

TM/LAM | Maputo | Mozambique = C9

Lao Airlines

QV/LAO | Vientiane | Laos = RDPL

LAN Airlines

LA/LAN | Santiago – Arturo Merino Benitez | Chile = CC

LAN Peru

LP/LPE | Lima | Peru = OB

LANExpress

LU/LXP | Santiago – Arturo Merino Benitez | Chile = CC

Lion Airlines

JT/LNI | Jakarta – Soekarno Hatta
International | Indonesia = PK

Lacsa

LR/LRC | San Jose – Juan Santamaria
| Costa Rica = TI

Livingston

LM/LVG | Milan – Malpensa | Italy = I

Lions Air AG

/LEU | Zurich | Switzerland = HB

Libyan Airlines

LN/LAA | Tripoli – Ben Gashair International
| Libya = 5A

Libyan Arab Air Cargo

/LCR | Tripoli – Ben Gashair International
| Libya = 5A

Lithuanian Airlines

TE/LIL | Vilnius | Lithuania = LY

Lotus Air

/TAS | Cairo International | Egypt = SU

LTE International Airways

XO/LTE | Palma de Mallorca | Spain = EC

LTU
Lufttransport Unternehmen

LT/LTU | Dusseldorf | Germany = D

LOT Polish Airlines

LO/LOT | Warsaw – Frederic Chopin | Poland = SP

Star Alliance tail

Luxair
Luxembourg Airlines

LG/LGL | Luxembourg | Luxembourg = LX

Lynden Air Cargo

L2/LYC | Anchorage International | USA = N

Lufthansa

LH/DLH | Frankfurt | Germany = D

Retro scheme

Mandala Airlines

RI/MDL | Jakarta – Soekarno Hatta
International | Indonesia = PK

Maersk Air

DM/DAN | Copenhagen – Kastrup
| Denmark =OY

MAI
Myanmar Airways International

S7-RGM

8M/ | Yangon | Myanmar/Burma = XY

Marsland Aviation

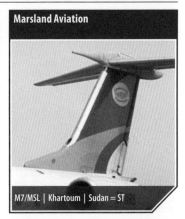

M7/MSL | Khartoum | Sudan = ST

Malmo Aviation

SE-

TF/SCW | Malmo – Sturup | Sweden = SE

Mandarin Airlines

AE/MDA | Taichung | China – Taiwan = B

Malev

HA-LM

MA/MAH | Budapest – Ferihegy | Hungary = HA

Maximus Air Cargo

/MXU | Abu Dhabi International | UAE = A6

Map Jet

Vienna | Austria = OE

Maverick Helicopters

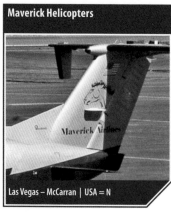

Las Vegas – McCarran | USA = N

Mahan Air

W5/IRM | Tehran – Imam Khomeini International | Iran = EP

Malaysia Airlines

MH/MAS | Kuala Lumpur | Malaysia = 9M

Martinair Holland

MP/MPH | Amsterdam – Schiphol | Holland = PH | Alternative tail markings

Merpati

MZ/MNA | Jakarta – Soekarno Hatta
International | Indonesia = PK

Medavia
Mediterranean Aviation Co.

N5/MDM | Malta – Luqa | Malta = 9H

MCHS Rossii

/SUM | Moscow – Domodedovo | Russia = RA

Mango

JE/MNO | Johannesburg International
| South Africa = ZS

Middle East Airlines

ME/MEA | Beirut | Lebanon = OD

Meridiana Fly

IG/EEZ | Olbia | Italy = I

Mexicana

MX/MXA | Mexico City | Mexico = XA/B/C

Alternative tail marks

Midwest Airlines

YX/MEP | Milwaukee – General Mitchell International | USA = N

MIAT
Mongolian Airlines

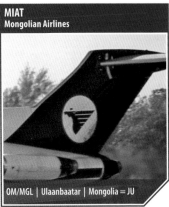

OM/MGL | Ulaanbaatar | Mongolia = JU

MNG Airlines

MB/MNB | Istanbul – Ataturk | Turkey = TC

Moldavian Airlines

2M/MDV | Chisinau | Moldova = ER

Motor Sich Airlines

M9/MSI | Zaporozhye | Ukraine = UR

Monarch Airlines

ZB/MON | London Luton | UK = G

Moscovia Airlines

Moscow – Zhukovsky | Russia = RA

Murray Aviation

N8/MUA | Detroit – Willow Run | USA = N

Montenegro Airlines

YM/MGX | Podgorica | Montenegro = 40

Neos

NO/NOS | Milan – Malpensa | Italy = I

Norwegian Air Shuttle

DY/NAX | Oslo | Norway = LN

Famous Scandinavians tail markings – Jenny Lind

Famous Scandinavians tail markings – Carl Larsson

Famous Scandinavians tail markings – André Bjerke

Nouvelair Tunisie

BJ/LBT | Monastir | Tunisia = TS

Nigerian Government

Abuja – Nnamdi Azikiwe International | Nigeria = 5N

Northwest Airlines

NW/NWA | Minneapolis/St. Paul | USA = N

Alternative tail marks

Nakanihon Airlines

NV/ | Nagoya | Japan = JA

Niki

HG/NLY | Vienna | Austria = OE

North American Airlines

NA/NAO | New York – JFK | USA = N

Nippon Cargo Airlines

KZ/NCA | Tokyo – Narita | Japan = JA

Nok Air

DD/NOK | Bangkok – Don Mueang
| Thailand = HS

Nordwind Airlines

N4/NWS | Moscow – Sheremetyevo
| Russia = RA

Oman Air

WY/OMA | Muscat – Seeb International
| Oman = A40

Alternative tail markings

OTL
Ostfriesische Lufttransport

OL/OLT | Emden | Germany = D

Orenair

R2/ORB | Orenburg – Tsentralny | Russia = RA

Olympic Air

OA/NOA | Athens – Eleftherios Venizelos
International | Greece = SX

Orbital Sciences

Bakersfield – Meadows Field | USA = N

Onur Air

8Q/OHY | Istanbul – Ataturk | Turkey = TC

Oriental Air Bridge

O3/ORC | Nagasaki | Japan = JA

Our Airline

ON/RON | Brisbane | Australia = VH

One-Two-GO

OG/OTG | Bangkok – Don Mueang
| Thailand = HS

Orient Thai Airlines

OX/OEA | Bangkok | Thailand = HS

Pluna

PU/PUA | Montevideo – Carrasco
| Uruguay = CX

Phuket Air

9R/VAP | Bangkok | Thailand = HS

Penair

KS/PEN | Anchorage International | USA = N

Polet Flight

YQ/POT | Ulyanovsk – Vostochny
| Russia = RA

PGA
Portugalia Airlines

NI/PGA | Lisbon | Portugal = CS

Pacific Eagle Aviation

Port McNeil | Canada = C

Pegasus Airlines

PC/PGT | Istanbul – Ataturk | Turkey = TC

Palmair

flypalmair.co.uk

Bournemouth | UK = G

Perm Airlines Company

RA-65751

P9/PGP | Perm – Bolshoe Savino
| Russia = RA

Pacific Coastal Airlines

C-F

8P/PCO | Vancouver International | Canada = C   Carrier has multi tail designs

Pantanal Linhas Aereas

P8/PTN | São Paulo – Congonhas
| Brazil = PP & PT

Pat Bay Air

C-FEGE

Victoria International | Canada = C

Polar Air Cargo

PO/PAC | New York – JFK | USA = N

PIA Pakistan International Airlines

PK/PIA | Karachi | Pakistan = AP

'Nature's Orchard' tail design

'The Silk Route' tail design

Pel-Air Aviation

/QWA | Brisbane International
| Australia = VH

Privatair

PTI & PTG | Geneva & Dusseldorf
| Switzerland = HB & Germany = D

Philippine Airlines

PR/PAL | Manila | Philippines = RP

Purolator
Kelowna Flightcraft

Mississauga | Canada = C

Qantas

QF/QFA | Sydney – Kingsford Smith
| Australia = VH

Royal Air Maroc

AT/RAM | Casablanca- Anfa | Morocco = CN

Qatar Airways

QR/QTR | Doha | Qatar = A7

Alternative tail logo

'Asian Games' special scheme

'Asian Games' special scheme

Rusline

/RLU | Moscow – Sheremetyevo | Russia = RA

Regal Air

Anchorage – Lake Hood Sea Plane Base
| USA = N

Regional Avia

Ekaterinburg – Koltsovo | Russia = RA

Royal Jet

/ROJ | Abu Dhabi International | UAE = A6

Rusair

/CGI | Moscow – Sheremetyevo | Russia = RA

Republic Airlines

YX/RPA | Chicago – O'Hare | USA = N

Rustair

Anchorage – Lake Hood Sea Plane Base | USA = N

Royal Nepal Airlines

RA/RNA | Kathmandu | Nepal = 9N

Rossiya

EI-DZH

FV/SDM | St Petersburg – Pulkovo
| Russia = RA

Royal Jordanian

JY-AYK

RJ/RJA | Amman – Queen Alia International
| Jordan = JY

Ryanair

FR/RYR | Dublin | Ireland = EI

Reem Air

V4/REK | Bishkek Manas | Kyrgyzstan = EX

Regional

YS/RAE | Nantes – Atlantique | France = F

REX
Regional Express

VH-SBA

ZL/RXA | Wagga Wagga | Australia = VH

Ryukyu Air Commuter

Okinawa – Naha | Japan = JA

Rovos Air

6P/ | Pretoria – Wonderboom
| South Africa = ZS

Rwandair

WB/RWD | Kigali | Rwanda = 9XR

Royal Brunei Airlines

BI/RBA | Bandar Seri Begawan | Brunei = V8

SAEP Servicios Aereos Especializados en Transportes Petroleros

/KSP | Bogota | Colombia = HK

Satena Servicio de Aeronavegacion a Territorios Nacionales

9N/NSE | Bogota | Colombia = HK

SAS
Scandinavian Airlines System

SK/SAS | Copenhagen/Stockholm/Oslo | Denmark = OY, Sweden = SE, Norway = LN

Retro scheme

SATA International

S4/RZO | Lisbon – Ponta Degada | Portugal = CS

Safair

FA/SFR | Johannesburg International | South Africa = ZS

South African Express

XZ/EXY | Johannesburg International | South Africa = ZS

Saudi Arabian VIP (Royal Flight)

Riyadh | Saudi Arabia = HZ

South African Airways

SA/SAA | Johannesburg International | South Africa = ZS

Sadelca
Sociedad Aerea del Caqueta

/SDK | Villavicencio | Colombia = HK

Saudi Arabian Airlines

SV/SVA | Riyadh | Saudi Arabia = HZ

SAM Sociedad Aeronautica de Medellin Consolidada

Medellin – Enrique Olaya Herrera | Colombia = HK

Searca
Servicio Aereo de Capurgana SA

Medellin – Enrique Olaya Herrera | Colombia = HK

Saga Airlines

H3/SGX | Istanbul – Ataturk | Turkey = TC

SCAT

DV/VSV | Shymkent | Kazakhstan = UP

Scot Airways

G-BWWT

CB/SAY | Cambridge | UK = G

Scenic Airlines

N14

YR/EGJ | Las Vegas – North | USA = N

Saltspring Air

C-FAOP

Saltspring Island – Ganges
Harbour Sea Plane Base | Canada = C

Seair Seaplanes

C-GURL

Vancouver International | Canada = C

Shanghai Airlines

FM/CSH | Shanghai – Hongqiao | China = B

Shandong Airlines

SC/CDG | Jinan – Yaoqiang International
| China = B

Shenzhen Airlines

ZH/CSZ | Shenzhen – Baoan | China = B

Silk Way Airlines

ZP/AZQ | Baku – Geidar Aliev International
| Azerbaijan = 4K

Singapore Airlines

SQ/SIA | Singapore – Changi | Singapore = 9V

Silkair

MI/SLK | Singapore – Changi | Singapore = 9V

Shortstop Jet Charter

Melbourne – Essendon | Australia = VH

Sharp Aviation

SH/ | Hamilton | Australia = VH

Sibir Airlines

Сибирь

S7/SBI | Novosibirsk – Tolmachevo
| Russia = RA

SkyExpress

VP-BFM

XW/SXR | Moscow – Vnukovo | Russia = RA

Sky Airline

CC-CTD

H2/SKU | Santiago – Arturo Merino Benitez
| Chile = CC

Sky Airlines

C-SKN

/SHY | Antalya | Turkey = TC

Smart Wings

QS/TVS | Prague – Ruzyne
| Czech Republic = OK

Skynet Asia Airways

LQ/SNJ | Miyazaki | Japan = JA

Special tail markings

Southwest Airlines

WN/SWA | Dallas – Love Field | USA = N

Special scheme

Skymark Airlines

BC/SKY | Tokyo – Haneda | Japan = JA

Sichuan Airlines

3U/CSC | Chengdu | China = B

Southern Air

9S/SOO | Hartford – Bradley International | USA = N

Spirit Airlines

NK/NKS | Fort Lauderdale – Hollywood International | USA = N

Sun Country Airlines

SY/SCX | Minneapolis/St. Paul International | USA = N

Syrian Arab Airlines

RB/SYR | Damascus | Syria = YK

SriLankan Airlines

UL/ALK | Colombo – Bandaranayike International | Sri Lanka = 4R

Star Flyer

7G/SFG | Kitakyushu | Japan = JA

Strategic Airlines

VC/AGC | Brisbane & Paris | Australia = VH & France = F

Star Airlines

SE/SEU | Paris – Charles De Gaulle | France = F

Surinam Airways

PY/SLM | Paramaribo – Zorg En Hoop | Surinam = PZ

Sonair Sarl

/SOR | Luanda | Angola = D2

Sudan Airways

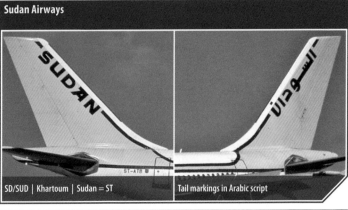

SD/SUD | Khartoum | Sudan = ST

Tail markings in Arabic script

Sprint Air

/SRN | Warsaw – Frederic Chopin | Poland = SP

Summit Air Charters

Yellowknife | Canada = C

Sun Express

XQ/SXS | Antalya | Turkey = TC

Sun-Air of Scandinavia

EZ/SUS | Billund | Denmark = OY

Swiss International Air Lines

LX/SWR | Zurich | Switzerland = HB

Swiftair SA

7J/SWT | Madrid – Barajas | Sprain = EC

Spanair

JK/JKK | Palma – Son Sant Joan | Spain = EC

S7 Airlines

S7/SBI | Novosibirsk – Tolmachevo | Russia = RA

SkyWest Airlines

OO/SKW | St. George Municipal | USA = N

Sierra Pacific Airlines

/SPA | Tucson International | USA = N

TACV
Transportes Aereos de Cabo Verde

VR/TCV | Praia | Cape Verde Islands = D4

TAP Portugal

TP/TAP | Lisbon | Portugal = CS

Tailwind Airlines

TI/TWI | Istanbul – Ataturk | Turkey = TC

TAME
Linea Aerea del Ecuador

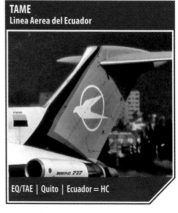

EQ/TAE | Quito | Ecuador = HC

Taerco
Taxi Aereo Colombiano

Villavicencio | Colombia = HK

Tatarstan

U9/TAK | Kazan | Russia = RA

TAAG – Angola Airlines

DT/DTA | Luanda | Angola = D2

Tajikistan Airlines

7J/TZK | Dushanbe | Tajikistan = EY

Tarom

RO/ROT | Bucharest – Henri Coanda
| Romania = YR

Taban Air

HH/TBM | Mashad | Iran = EP

Tarhan Tower Airlines

/TTH | Istanbul – Ataturk | Turkey = TC

TACA International Airlines

TA/TAI | San Salvador – Comalapa
International | El Salvador = YS

TACA Peru

TO/TPU | Lima | Peru = OB

TAM – Linhas Aereas

JJ/TAM | Sao Paulo – Congonhas
| Brazil = PP & PT

TBM

Tulare | USA = N

Titan Airways

ZT/AWC | London – Stansted | UK = G

Tiger Airways

TR/TGW | Singapore – Changi | Singapore = 9V

Thai Airways International

TG/THA | Bangkok | Thailand = HS

Thai AirAsia

FD/AIQ | Bangkok | Thailand = HS

Thomson Airways

BY/TOM | London – Luton | UK = G

Thomas Cook Airlines

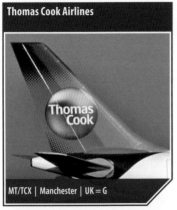

MT/TCX | Manchester | UK = G

TNT (Pan-Air)

PV/PNR | Madrid – Barajas | Spain = EC

Transwest Air

GCTG

9T/ABS | Prince Albert | Canada = C

Transavia Airlines

HV/TRA | Amsterdam – Schiphol
| Holland = PH

Transaero Airlines

VP-BQC

UN/TSO | Moscow – Domodedovo | Russia = RA

TRI-MG Intra Asia

GY/TMG | Jakarta – Halim | Indonesia = PK

TransAsia Airways

GE/TNA | Taipei Sung Shan
| China – Taiwan = B

Transnorthern

N30TN

/TNV | Anchorage International | USA = N

Trans Oriente

Villavicencio | Colombia = HK

Turkmenistan Airlines

A005

T5/TUA | Ashgabat | Turkmenistan = EZ

Travel Service

OK-TVD

QS/TVS | Prague – Ruzyne | Czech Republic = OK

Special tail markings

Turkish Airlines

TK/THY | Istanbul – Ataturk | Turkey = TC

Retro scheme

Turkuaz Airlines

/TRK | Istanbul – Ataturk | Turkey = TC

Turan Air

3T/URN | Baku – Geidar Aliev International | Azerbaijan = 4K

TUIfly

X3/HLX | Hannover | Germany = D

Special tail scheme

Tyrolean Airways

VO/TYR | Innsbruck | Austria = OE

Tunisair

TU/TAR | Tunis – Cartage | Tunisia = TS

UTair

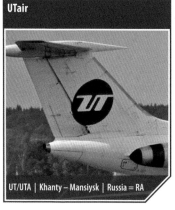

UT/UTA | Khanty – Mansiysk | Russia = RA

Ukraine Air Alliance

/UKL | Kiev | Ukraine = UR

Ukraine International Airlines

PS/AUI | Kiev – Borispol | Ukraine = UR

United Airlines

UA/UAL | Chicago – O'Hare | USA = N

Ural Airlines

U6/SVR | Ekaterinburg – Koltsovo
| Russia = RA

UPS
United Parcel Service

5X/UPS | Louisville International | USA = N

US Airways

US/AWE | Charlotte – Douglas
International | USA = N

USA 3000

U5/GWY | Philadelphia International
| USA = N

Virgin America

VX/VRD | San Francisco International
| USA = N

Virgin Blue Airlines

DJ/VOZ | Brisbane International
| Australia = VH

Virgin Atlantic Airways

VS/VIR | London Gatwick | UK = G

V Australia

/VAU | Sydney – Kingsford Smith
| Australia = VH

Vim Avia

NN/MOV | Moscow – Domodedovo
| Russia = RA

Vancouver Island Air

/VIA | Campbell River | Canada = C

Varig
VRG Linhas Aereas

RG/VRN | Rio de Janeiro | Brazil = PP & PT

Special markings

Volga – Dnepr Airlines

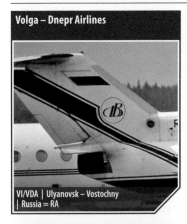

VI/VDA | Ulyanovsk – Vostochny | Russia = RA

VistaJet

/VJS | Salzburg | Austria = OE

VIA
Air VIA Bulgarian Airways

VL/VIM | Sofia | Bulgaria = LZ

VIP
Vuelos Internos Privados

V6/VUR | Quito | Ecuador = HC

Viking Airlines

4P/VIK | Stockholm | Sweden = SE

VisionAir

V2/RBY | Las Vegas – North | USA = N

Valuair

VF/VLU | Singapore – Changi | Singapore = 9V

Vueling Airlines

VY/VLG | Barcelona – El Prat | Spain = EC

Vietnam Airlines

VN/HVN | Hanoi | Vietnam = VN

VLM

VG/VLM | Antwerp – Deurne | Belgium = OO

Vladivostok Air

XF/VLK | Vladivostok | Russia = RA

Wideroe's Flyveselskap

WF/WIF | Bodo | Norway = LN

West Wind Aviation

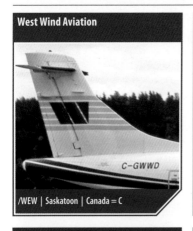

/WEW | Saskatoon | Canada = C

Wizz Air

W6/WZZ | Budapest – Ferihegy | Hungary = HA

WestJet

WS/WJA | Calgary International | Canada = C

West Coast Air

80/ | Vancouver International | Canada = C

Warbelows Air

4W/WAV | Fairbanks International | USA = N

World Airways

WO/WOA | Atlanta – Hartsfield Jackson | USA = N

WDL Aviation

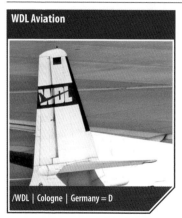

/WDL | Cologne | Germany = D

Windjet

IV/JET | Catania –Fontanarossa | Italy = I

XL Airways France

SE/XLF | Paris – Charles De Gaulle | France = F

Xinjiang General Aviation

Shihezi | China = B

Xiamen Airlines

MF/CXA | Xiamen | China = B

Yakutia

R3/SYL | Yakutsk International | Russia = RA

Yamal

YC/LLM | Salekhard | Russia = RA

Yemenia – Yemen Airways Corp

IY/IYE | Sana'a | Yemen = 70

1time Airline

1T/RNX | Johannesburg International | South Africa = ZS

224 Flight Unit State Airlines

/TTF | Bryansk 2 | Russia = RA

Countries/Registration letters

Country	Code	Country	Code	Country	Code	Country	Code
Afghanistan	YA	Ecuador	HC	Madagascar	5R	Slovenia	S5
Albania	ZA	Egypt	SU	Malawi	7Q	Solomon Islands	H4
Algeria	7T	El Salvador	YS	Malaysia	9M	South Africa	ZS
Andorra	C3	Equatorial Guinea	3C	Maldives	8Q	Spain	EC
Angola	D2	Eritrea	E3	Mali	TZ	Sri Lanka	4B
Anguilla	VP-A	Estonia	ES	Malta	9H	St Lucia	J6
Antigua & Barbuda	V2	Ethopia	ET	Marshall Islands	V7	St Vincent & Grenadines	J8
Argentina	LV	Falkland Islands	VP-F	Mauritania	5T	Sudan	ST
Armenia	EK	Fiji	DQ	Mauritius	3B	Suriname	PZ
Aruba	P4	Finland	OH	Mexico	XA/XB/XC	Sweden	SE
Australia	VH	France	F	Micronesia	V6	Switzerland	HB
Austria	OE	Gabon	TR	Moldova	ER	Syria	YK
Azerbaijan	4K	Gambia	C5	Monaco	3A	Tajikistan	EY
Bahamas	C6	Georgia	4L	Mongolia	JU	Tanzania	5H
Bahrain	A9C	Germany	D	Montenegro	4O	Thailand	HS
Bangladesh	S2	Ghana	9G	Montserrat	VP-M	Togo	5V
Barbados	8P	Greece	SX	Morocco	CN	Tonga	A3
Belarus	EW	Guatemala	TG	Mozambique	C9	Trinidad & Tobago	9Y
Belgium	OO	Guinea	3X	Myanmar/Burma	XY	Tunisia	TS
Belize	V3	Guyana	8R	Namibia	V5	Turkey	TC
Benin	TY	Haiti	HH	Nepal	9N	Turkmenistan	EZ
Bermuda	VP-B	Honduras	HR	Netherlands	PH	Turks & Caicos Islands	VQ-T
Bhutan	A5	Hong Kong	B-H	Netherland Antilles	PJ	Uganda	5X
Bolivia	CP	Hungary	HA	New Zealand	ZK	Ukraine	UR
Bosnia & Herzrgovina	E7	Iceland	TF	Nicaragua	YN	United Arab Emirates	A6
Botswana	A2	India	VT	Niger	5U	United Kingdom	G
Brazil	PP & PT	Indonesia	PK	Nigeria	5N	Uruguay	CX
British Virgin Islands	VP-L	Iran	EP	Norway	LN	USA	N
Brunei	V8	Iraq	YI	Oman	A4O	Uzbekistan	UK
Bulgaria	LZ	Ireland	EI	Pakistan	AP	Vanuatu	YJ
Burkina Faso	XT	Isle of Man	M	Palestine	SU-Y	Vatican City	HV
Cambodia	XU	Israel	4X	Panama	HP	Venezuela	YV
Cameroon	TJ	Italy	I	Papua New Guinea	P2	Vietnam	VN
Canada	C	Ivory Coast	TU	Paraguay	ZP	Yemen	7O
Cape Verde Islands	D4	Jamaica	6Y	Peru	OB	Zambia	9J
Cayman Islands	VP-C	Japan	JA	Philippines	RP	Zimbabwe	Z
Central African Republic	TL	Jordan	JY	Poland	SP		
Chad	TT	Kazakhstan	UP	Portugal	CS		
Chile	CC	Kenya	5Y	Qatar	A7		
China & Taiwan	B	Kiribati	T3	Republic of the Congo	TN		
Colombia	HK	Korea -South	HL	Romania	YR		
Comoros	D6	Korea -North	P	Russia	RA		
Cook Islands	E5	Kuwait	9K	Rwanda	9XR		
Costa Rica	TI	Kyrgyzstan	EX	Samoa	5W		
Croatia	9A	Laos	RDPL	San Marino	T7		
Cuba	CU	Latvia	YL	Sao Tome & Principe	S9		
Cyprus	5B	Lebanon	OD	Saudi Arabia	HZ		
Czech Rebublic	OK	Lesotho	7P	Senegal	6V		
Democratic Republic of Congo	9Q	Libya	5A	Serbia	YU		
Denmark	OY	Lithuania	LY	Seychelles	S7		
Djibouti	J2	Luxembourg	LX	Sierra Leone	9L		
Dominican Republic	HI	Macau	B-M	Singapore	9V		
		Macedonia	Z3	Solvakia	OM		

3A	Monaco	B-M	Macau	JU	Mongolia	TU	Ivory Coast
3B	Mauritius	C	Canada	JY	Jordan	TY	Benin
3C	Equatorial Guinea	C3	Andorra	LN	Norway	TZ	Mali
3X	Guinea	C5	Gambia	LV	Argentina	UK	Uzbekistan
4K	Azerbaijan	C6	Bahamas	LX	Luxembourg	UP	Kazakhstan
4L	Georgia	C9	Mozambique	LY	Lithuania	UR	Ukraine
4O	Montenegro	CC	Chile	LZ	Bulgaria	V2	Antigue & Barbuda
4R	Sri Lanka	CN	Morocco	M	Isle of Man	V3	Belize
4X	Israel	CP	Bolivia	N	USA	V5	Namibia
5A	Libya	CS	Portugal	OB	Peru	V6	Micronesia
5B	Cyprus	CU	Cuba	OD	Lebanon	V7	Marshall Islands
5H	Tanzania	CX	Uruguay	OE	Austria	V8	Brunei
5N	Nigeria	D	Germany	OH	Finland	VH	Australia
5R	Madagascar	D2	Angola	OK	Czech Republic	VN	Vietnam
5T	Mauritania	D4	Cape Verde Islands	OM	Slovakia	VP-A	Anguilla
5U	Niger	D6	Comoros	OO	Belgium	VP-B	Bermuda
5V	Togo	DQ	Fiji	OY	Denmark	VP-C	Cayman Islands
5W	Samoa	E3	Eritrea	P	Korea - North	VP-F	Falkland Islands
5X	Uganda	E5	Cook Islands	P2	Papua New Guinea	VP-L	British Virgin
5Y	Kenya	E7	Bosnia &	P4	Aruba		Islands
6V	Senegal		Herzegovina	PH	Netherlands	VP-M	Montserrat
6Y	Jamaica	EC	Spain	PJ	Netherland Antillies	VQ-T	Turks & Caicos
7O	Yemen	EI	Ireland	PK	Indonesia		Islands
7P	Lesotho	EK	Armenia	PP & PT	Brazil	VT	India
7Q	Malawi	EP	Iran	PZ	Suriname	XA/XB/XC	Mexico
7T	Algeria	ER	Moldova	RA	Russia	XT	Burkina Faso
8P	Barbados	ES	Estonia	RDPL	Laos	XU	Cambodia
8Q	Maldives	ET	Ethiopia	RP	Philippines	XY	Myanmar/Burma
8R	Guyana	EW	Belarus	S2	Bangladesh	YA	Afghanistan
9A	Croatia	EX	Kyrgyzstan	S5	Slovinia	YI	Iraq
9G	Ghana	EY	Tajikistan	S7	Seychelles	YJ	Vanuatu
9H	Malta	EZ	Turkmenistan	S9	Sao Tome	YK	Syria
9J	Zambia	F	France		& Principe	YL	Latvia
9K	Kuwait	G	United Kingdom	SE	Sweden	YN	Nicaragua
9L	Sierra Leone	H4	Solomon Islands	SP	Poland	YR	Romania
9M	Malaysia	HA	Hungary	ST	Sudan	YS	El Salvador
9N	Nepal	HB	Switzerland	SU	Egypt	YU	Serbia
9Q	Democratic	HC	Ecuador	SU-Y	Palestine	YV	Venezuela
	Republic of Congo	HH	Haiti	SX	Greece	Z	Zimbabwe
9V	Singapore	HI	Dominican	T3	Kiribati	Z3	Macedonia
9XR	Rwanda		Republic	T7	San Marino	ZA	Albania
9Y	Trinidad & Tobago	HK	Colombia	TC	Turkey	ZK	New Zealand
A2	Botswana	HL	Korea - South	TF	Iceland	ZP	Paraguay
A3	Tonga	HP	Panama	TG	Guatemala	ZS	South Africa
A40	Oman	HR	Honduras	TI	Costa Rica		
A5	Bhutan	HS	Thailand	TJ	Cameroon		
A6	United Arab	HZ	Saudi Arabia	TL	Central African		
	Emirates	I	Italy		Republic		
A7	Qatar	J2	Djibouti	TN	Republic of the		
A9C	Bahrain	J6	St Lucia		Congo		
AP	Pakistan	J8	St Vincent &	TR	Gabon		
B	China (both)		Grenadines	TS	Tunisia		
B-H	Hong Kong	JA	Japan	TT	Chad		